WHAT ARE STOCKS?

Understanding the Stock Market

Finance Book for Kids

Children's Money & Saving Reference

BABY PROFESSOR

EDUCATION KIDS

Speedy Publishing LLC

40 E. Main St. #1156

Newark, DE 19711

www.speedypublishing.com

Copyright 2017

Stocks represent ownership of a company and each share of a stock is worth a certain amount or percentage of the company. If a company has a total of 100 shares, each share would represent 1% ownership in the company. If you own at least 51 shares, you then own majority of the company.

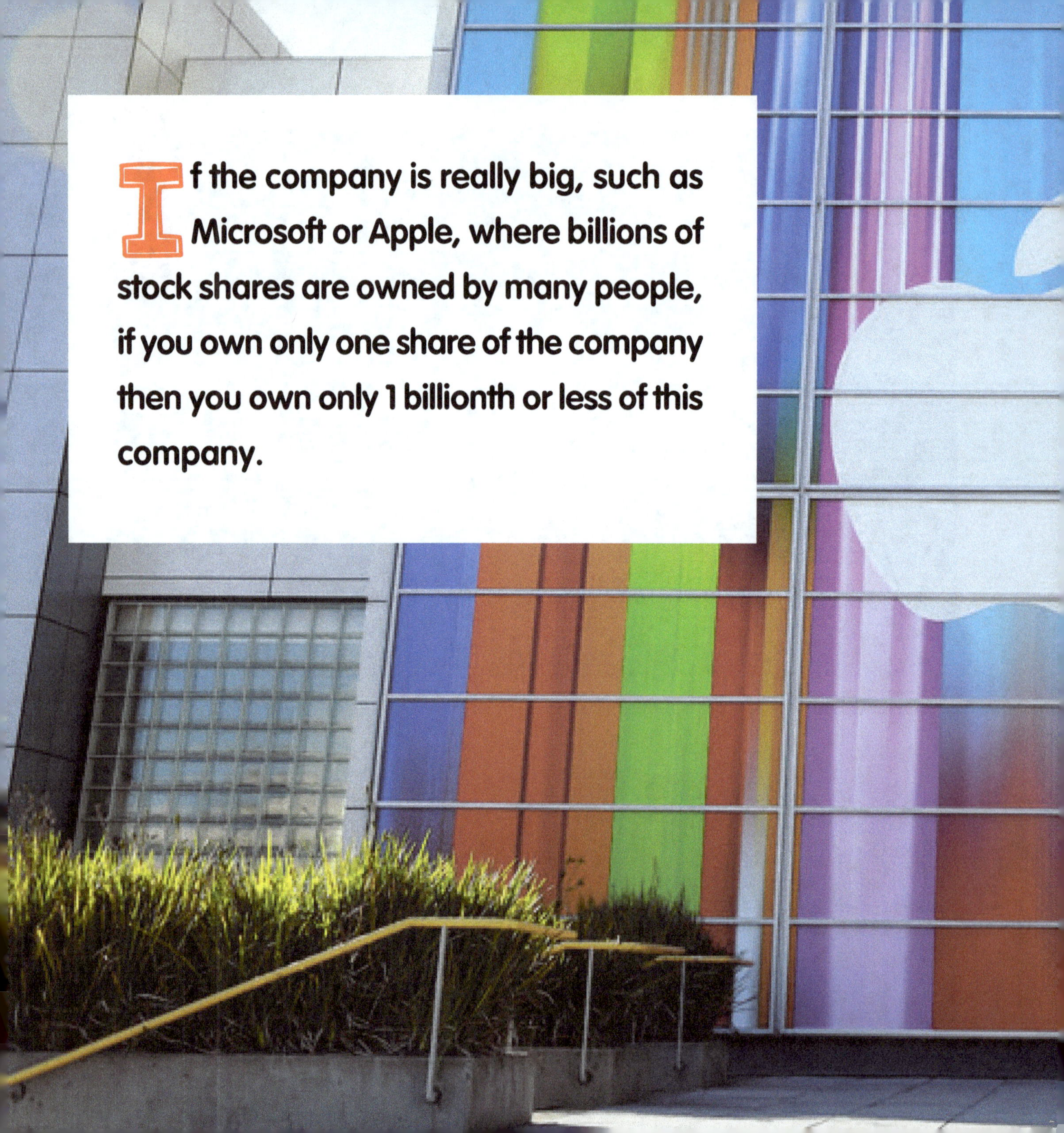
If the company is really big, such as Microsoft or Apple, where billions of stock shares are owned by many people, if you own only one share of the company then you own only 1 billionth or less of this company.

Yerba Buena Center for the Arts

SELLING STOCKS
Services
195K
Technolo
73.39K
Financial
SELL
132.96
0.27%
0.65
238.74
1.41%
27.45
0.20%
0.05
67.69

WHY DOES A COMPANY SELL STOCK?

Most of the time they sell their stock in order to raise money for expansion. If they sell stock, then they do not need to take a loan out and pay interest, they merely sell a part of their company. The funds received by selling stock is used to do things such as hiring new employees, developing new products, and building new buildings.

WHAT IS THE STOCK EXCHANGE?

The place where stocks are bought and sold is referred to as a stock exchange. There are many stock exchanges around the world, including two of the largest exchanges in the United States; the NASDAQ and the New York Stock Exchange, both located in New York City.

DISPLAY OF STOCK MARKET QUOTES

Fast Food

YOUR SANDWICH SHOP

Suppose you are the owner of sandwich shop that is very successful and everyone loved to eat there and .you made a ton of money. Each year, your sandwich shop has made approximately $80,000 and so you decided to open nine additional shops throughout the country.

With ten shops, you would now be making **$800,000** profit. But, you realize that it will cost a lot of money to open the nine additional shops.

Obtaining a loan from a bank would be one option, and another option would be selling stock in your business.

So, after thinking about these options, you have deciding to sell stock and sold 50% of your company to people with shares of stock. This provided you with the funds needed to open the nine additional shops.

STOCK EXCHANGE CHART

At year's end, you might reward your investors with 50% of the profits in the form of dividends. If all the new shops were as profitable as the original shop, they would receive $400,000 from you, which leaves you with $400,000.

Even though you did not make all of the money, you made more than you did when you only had the one shop.

MAN MONITORING HIS STOCKS INVESTMENT

INVESTING

Many people invest in the market because there is potential for higher returns rather than the interest you received from a bank. However, the market is riskier than the bank. If you invest in the market, you could double your money in only a few years which is a much better return than the small percent of interest you receive from the bank.

However, if the market crashes, you could lose all of your money. The government guarantees your money that is held in the bank. You may not get a great return, but at least you won't lose it.

SOME LOSE AND SOME GAIN WHEN INVESTING IN THE STOCK MARKET

BEAR AND BULL ON THE STOCK EXCHANGE.

WHAT IS THE DIFFERENCE BETWEEN THE BEAR MARKET AND THE BULL MARKET?

Bear Market or Bull Market are terms people use when describing the present state of the market. If the values of the stocks are falling and people are feeling negative about the market's future, this is referred to as a Bear Market. If the values of the stocks are rising and people are feeling positive about the market's future, this is referred to as a Bull Market.

RISK VS. REWARD

There is risk to most investments and you might end up in the future with less money than you had today. Some are more risky than other, but typically the more of a risk that you are willing to take, the more money you might make.

REWARD

RISK

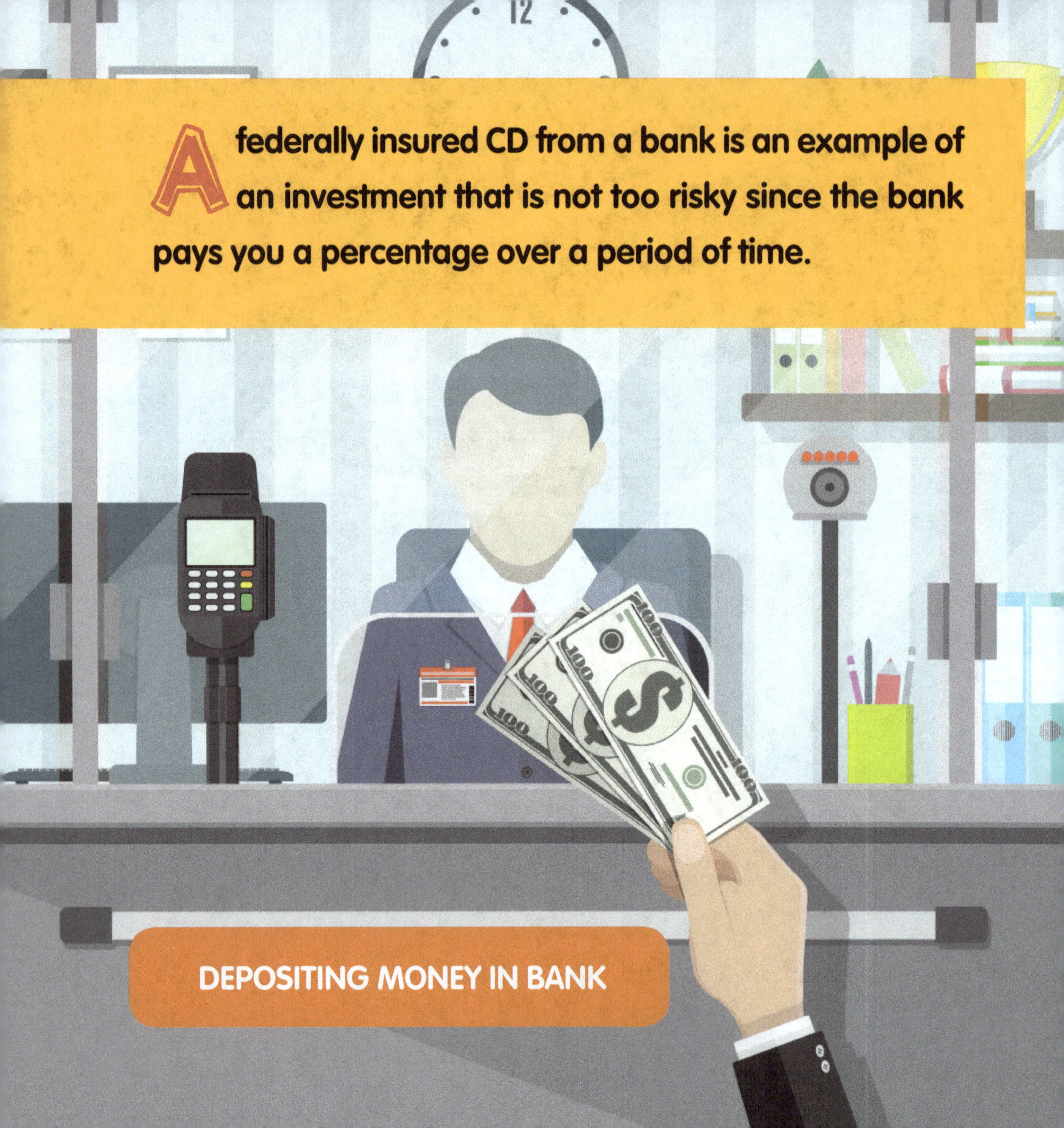

A federally insured CD from a bank is an example of an investment that is not too risky since the bank pays you a percentage over a period of time.

DEPOSITING MONEY IN BANK

ven it goes out of business, your money should be insured by the federal government. While this sounds like a great idea, CDs only pay a low percent each year, which is not a great investment return.

31,246.04
(+270.78)
26,275.30
(+7.62)
30,463.58
342.71
(+2.85)
60.44
60.30
511.22
(+45.49)
598.71
685.65
233.88
(-75.07)
142.09
154.12
(-7.84)
33.13
(-76.72)
(+18.08)
93.52
(-57.53)
75.41
(-19.36)
132.89
(+76.22)
220.19
143,653.64
(+0.68)
150,028.94
(+4.44)
156,015.25
142,684.54
726.98
741.27
48.64
50.44
16,579.05

Investing in stock of a new technology company would be a riskier example of an investment. Your money might go up a lot over the next few years if the company does well. However, should the company go out of business, the stock would become worthless and you will lose all of your money.

TYPES OF INVESTMENTS

There are many different forms of investments and some of the more common ones are listed here:

Stocks: Stocks represent ownership of a company, including companies such as Apple, Walmart, and Coca-Cola. You hope that the company will grow and be profitable. As the value of the company rises, your money will also grow.

MAN CHECKING HIS STOCKS
SELL
BUY
Financial report

Mutual Funds: Mutual funds are similar to stocks, but a mutual fund is representation of a group of stocks. This way, you can invest in several different stocks without having to purchase a bunch of individual stocks.

Bonds

Bonds: Bonds are similar to loans. When you purchase a bond, you're lending your money to the government or to a company. While bonds might pay a higher interest than a bank account, they also come along with additional risks.

INVESTMENT
INFOGRAPHICS

42%

INVESTORS

Mirum est notare quam litta gothica, quam nuncmazim placerat facer est notare

23,768,000

VALUES

Mazim placerat facer poss assum typi non habent

8,146,000

FUNDS

Claritas est etiam proces sus dynamicus, qui

76%
SAVINGS
Eodem modo typi, qui nu
nobis videntur parum cla
fiant sollemnes in futu

2,435,000
PERIOD
Lorem ipsum dolor sit parum
amet, consectetuer

3,723,000
GOLD
uis autem vel eum iriure ipsum
dolor in hendrerit congue

83%
STOCKS
Eleifend option congueno
nihil imperdiet doming

Real Estate: Many people chose to invest in real estate, such as land or buildings. Purchasing their home is the largest investment most people make.

Gold: Often used as an investment are precious metals, such as gold.

A COUPLE AFTER A SUCCESSFUL MEETING
WITH THEIR FINANCIAL ADVISOR.

SHOULD I DIVERSIFY MY INVESTMENTS?

Most financial advisors instruct their clients to diversify, which means investing in various areas. Instead of putting your money into only one stock, they suggest that you invest in various types of investments, including bonds, stocks and mutual funds.

THE STOCK MARKET CRASH OF 1929

One of the worst crashes of the market in United States' history was the Stock Market Crash of 1929. Stock values fell dramatically at the end of October and most people ended up losing their savings as well as their homes.

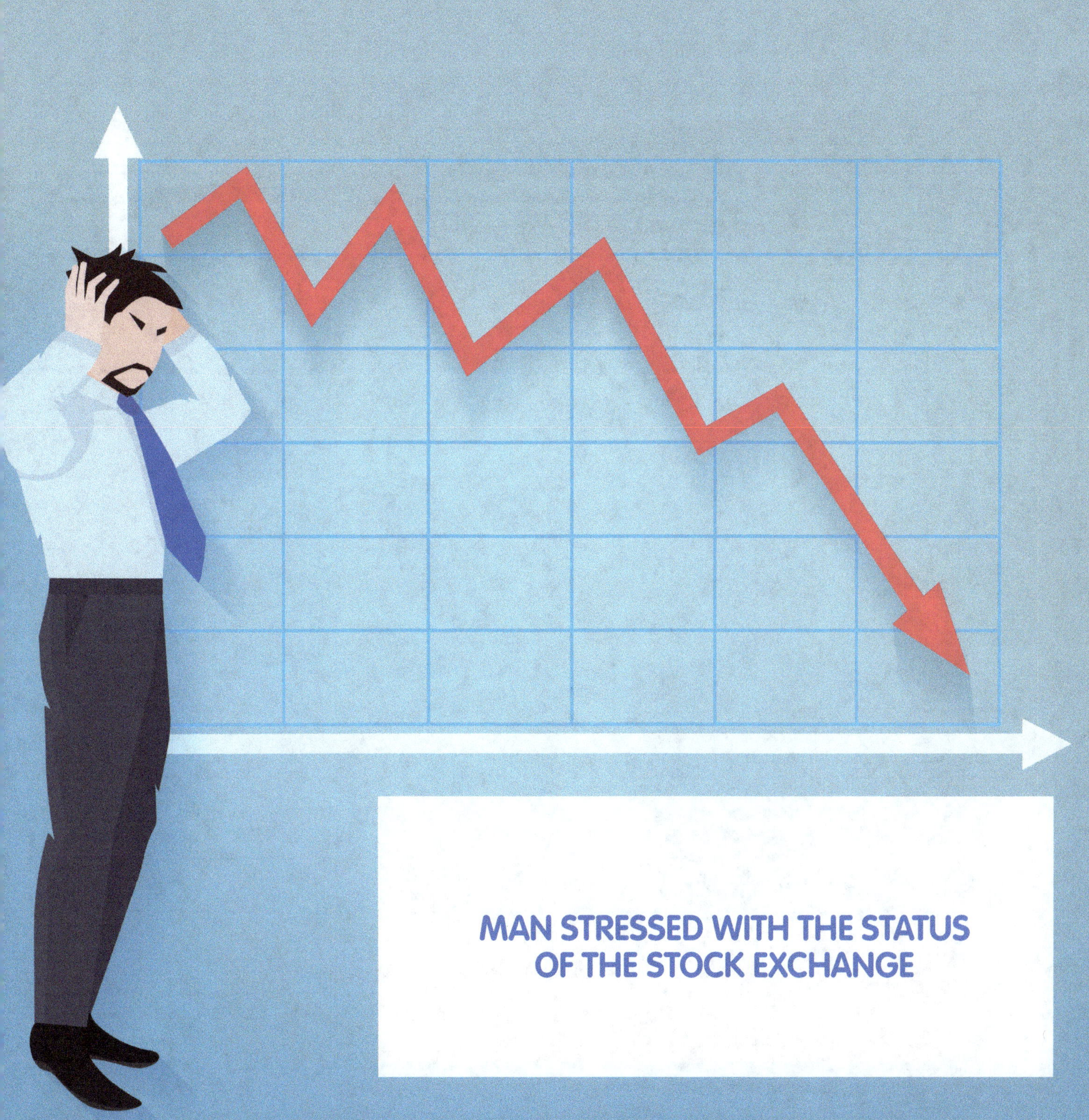
MAN STRESSED WITH THE STATUS
OF THE STOCK EXCHANGE

UNEMPLOYED MEN WAITING OUTSIDE
A DEPRESSION SOUP KITCHEN OPENED
IN CHICAGO BY AL CAPONE

usinesses had to lay off their employees or file for bankruptcy. This signaled the beginning of the Great Depression that ended up lasting more than ten years.

BEFORE THE CRASH

Also known as the "Roaring Twenties", the 1920s were a time of business speculation and economic boom. New industries including radios and autos were changing the culture and landscape of America.

1920
RETRO
MOTORS

<p>eople believed that everyone was going to become rich and that the economy would not stop growing. This optimism resulted in wild speculation with the market.

The stock market had grown by 600% between 1921 and 1929, and the Dow Jones Industrial Average rose from 63 to 381 points.

LEGAL TENDER
UBLIC AND PRIVATE
Jones Industrial Average
9500
9000
8500
WASHINGTON
ONE DOLLAR

THE CRASH

The market's crazy growth, however, was not based on reality and the economy would not be able to continue to grow at this rate forever. The economy started slowing down in 1929. Towards October's end, people started selling huge amounts of stock as panic gripped the market. October 28th and 29th were the worst two days as values fell 23%. These days are referred to as "Black Monday" and "Black Tuesday".

AFTER THE CRASH

The market was not able to recover, even though it tried. Over only a period of a few months, the market had fallen approximately 40% and many investors had lost everything. However, it wasn't until summertime of 1932 that it reached bottom, falling 89% from its peak. Billions were erased and the country had now entered a deep economic depression.

MANY PEOPLE LOST THEIR JOBS

STOCK MARKET

MAJOR CAUSES OF THE CRASH

There were several reasons for the stock market crash. Some of the major causes are listed here:

People buying stocks on credit: People started borrowing money to purchase stocks, referred to as a "margin". Once the market started falling, they had to quickly sell their stocks to pay their debts. This resulted in a domino effect and more and more people ended up having to sell.

Wild speculation: The market was growing too fast and stocks became overvalued.

The economy: There was a slowdown of the economy but the market did not reflect this. The market continued rising despite the signs of the struggling economy.

THE GREAT DEPRESSION

The Great Depression started with the crash of the market and lasted ten years, until 1939. It was during this time period that unemployment increased to about 25%, banks across the country were failing, and thousands of businesses were going bankrupt. Even though the crash of the stock market wasn't the only reason for the Great Depression, it had a major impact.

FAMILY LEAVING THEIR HOME
19 CALIFORNIA 34
6C 12 99

US ECONOMY SLOWLY RECOVERING FROM
THE GREAT ECONOMIC DEPRESSION
1950'S
1929

WHEN DID THE MARKET RECOVER?

In 1932, the market had reached peak bottom and proceeded to make a slight recovery. It was not able to make a complete recovery until the mid-1950s. There is a lot to think about when you are ready to invest your hard-earned money. Do you want it safe at a bank and receive a low return, or do you want to invest in stocks and possibly get a great return on your money?

or additional information about stocks and investing your money, you can visit your local library, research the internet, and ask questions of your teachers, family, and friends.

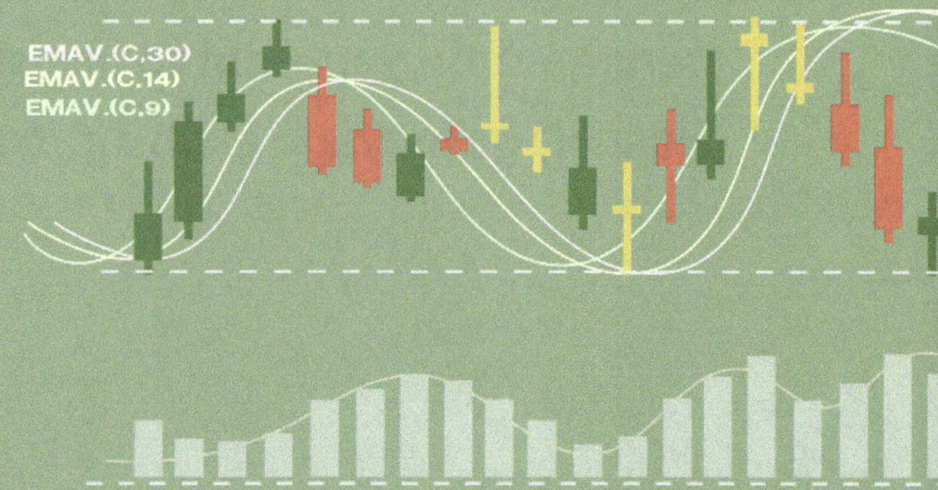

Buy
Resistance
Support
Vol

Visit
BABY PROFESSOR
EDUCATION KIDS
www.BabyProfessorBooks.com
to download Free Baby Professor eBooks
and view our catalog of new and exciting
Children's Books

www.ingramcontent.com/pod-product-compliance
Lightning Source LLC
Chambersburg PA
CBHW081148180726
48003CB00026B/2937